BREAD

Christina Gallegos

A celebration of successful miracles collides with a grieving Jesus, as hunger rises and demands to be fed.

Patience runs thin as resources are scarce, yet the people won't go home.

How can God be generous with so many empty pockets?

BREAD

Christina Gallegos

Exploring the depth of teaching on the miracle of Bread & fish

Mark 6:30-43

Bread. Fresh out of the oven on a cold day, warming the toes, spreading smiles of joy as rich butter is slathered on every bite.

Bread, a fundamental staple in nearly every pantry across the world, dating back to the beginning of Ages.

Baked, fried, flat, fluffy, soft, dense, made from fields of grain harvested in peak season. Bread, a universal food easily recognized by nearly every nation.

Simple, unimpressive bread. Yet Jesus chooses bread for a great miracle of feeding empty souls.

Together, we'll explore bread in ways that will beckon you to take and eat as much as you want.

Come, enjoy some Bread!

ISBN: 978-0-578-64454-7

Also by Christina Gallegos

The Goat Climbs High

A children's book about not feeling very special

The Tree Stands Firm

A children's book of never giving up

Upcoming release

Life w/ Boys

We are all hungry for a little more Bread

Contents

Just for you...

I really want you to grab hold of this study as if you could see yourself walking in the shoes of the disciples, feel their struggle, maybe even smell their sweat as they walk daily trying to figure out Who this Jesus is. Everyday people with dreams & ambitions just like you and I, vastly different yet with a common problem: hunger. Deep, down nitty-gritty hunger of the soul.

We'll explore a grief-struck Jesus meeting up with hoopla-makin' disciples full of wonderful miracles setting out for a little R&R on the Galilean shoreline. As interruptions don't meet expectations and thick-headed skulls refuse to see the simplicity of the lesson, the short list becomes rather empty. Unable to create the miracle themselves, the disciples are left scrambling for solutions that give way for Jesus to step up to the plate. A menial offering of poor man's bread, barely enough to feed a family, let alone an enormous crowd. Such a small, perhaps embarrassing, amount is placed in Jesus' Hands. The hunger builds as the miracles run dry.

Can the impossible happen when the bottom of the barrel has been scraped while lounging around a lonely seaside mountainside?

INTERRUPTED

"Calling the 12 to him, he sent them out two by two and gave them authority over evil spirits."

"They went out and preached that people should repent. They drove out many demons and anointed many sick people with oil and healed them."

"The apostles gathered around Jesus and reported to him all they had done & taught. Then, because so many people were coming and going that they did not even have a chance to eat."

Mark 6:7 & 12-13

High fives followed by walloping good-natured back slaps. Faces filled with, "Can you believe it?!", moments. The disciples clamor over one another, interrupting each other, full of conversation, eager to share with their Master, their inspiring great Teacher, all that they had been able to do.

1

More than half of the batch of rowdy men were sun-bronzed from the seashore of burly hands and arms fashioned as logs. These men were strong, salt of the earth kind of guys. A few others were a bit more refined, refusing to touch grimy rags of salted dust. Educated, these men possessed strength of mind, they were invited to many tables and had social connections of political power. A mixed batch indeed. A thug, a doctor, everyday fishermen, business owners, a professional extortionist, a completely gullible baby-faced Nathanael, along with a dedicated religious follower of John the Baptist from Andrew; nearly half of them are from the same hometown where everyone knows your name. Included were two sets of brothers, some impulsive while others had a reputation of wreaking havoc on the town seashore. There could not be a more ragamuffin group of men than these that had chosen to follow Jesus by the beckoning words of, "Come, follow me."

"Jesus! This demon-looking thing was staring at me, man, it was freaking me out, I didn't know what we were going to do. But my bro here, yeah, he's crazy, he went right up to that demon thing and told it to get out! The dude's body started flopping around on the ground and this white foamy junk started oozing out and I was like, "man, we gotta get out of here!" But nah, my boy John here, he tells me hold on, let's see what's gonna happen. Jesus, it was like the craziest thing, the guy went all stiff like I thought he died or something and then suddenly, he gets up off the ground smiling saying he's feeling better. What da what?! Dude, can you believe that? I ain't never seen anything like it!"

Another disciple pushes his way forward in country boy fashion, "well, that ain't nuthin'. Ya' see, that there town had some kind of cattle disease going through, people were dropping like fleas on a dog and I reached in my pocket, pulled out that special lightening oil You gave us and every person I touched on the forehead got suddenly better. I don't know what You're putting in that there special anointin' oil, Jesus, but it sure was a sight to see!"

"Oh yeah, well check this out," enters the Thug fighting for his claim to fame, "the magic is in the juice! Yo' man, my homey here, juicy fruit, stood up in the town square and dropped a fat beat. It was like dope, people came out from everywhere, started dancin' and havin' a good time. They gave us so much food and every time we were like, "Bam", people said they were healed! It was like Pop, Drop & Lock it goin' on everywhere!"

12 men, behaving like children released on a sunny playground after a week of rain. Not one seems to notice Jesus' quiet demise.

Their Teacher patiently listens to each story spilling forth, smiles & laughter with mind-blowing gestures abound. Contagious excitement of their road trip details spilled forth like crashing waves, pummeling the great Leaders ears of miracles and healings. They had never felt so empowered! In their excitement, they overlook a quiet & withdrawn Jesus. They interrupt Jesus.

Curious bystanders walk in and out the door, while others shove their way in for a closer look. The stories spill from the disciple's lips as they recount every God-given miracle of healing, every sermon preached in local towns. So many stories from 12 men, the day grew long as the bellies began to growl for nourishment. Fueled by energy drinks, they continue their non-stop gab about all that they had done.

In the quietness of His thoughts, Jesus wonders if the disciples remember the importance of their staffs on their journey. Jesus interrupts them, saying, "Come away with me."

At this very moment, while Jesus' disciples return from an all-time high of incredible miracles, full of adrenaline and excitement, they seem not to notice a very quiet Jesus.

Read Matthew 14:1-13

Quite literally, Jesus had just received the news that his close cousin John the Baptist had been unfairly murdered. The news either reached Him at the precise moment the disciples blew back into town or just shortly before. This is a grief-struck Jesus. In complete humanity, His response is to withdraw, try to process what just happened, have some quiet to clear His thoughts. Jesus' personal life is interrupted.

John the Baptist was his childhood friend, they would have shared meals of bread together, chased each other with sticks as children, applauded each other's first chin hairs. These men were once children from the same district, their mothers chattering for hours as they played hide-n-go-seek. These men also knew the calling in their lives, to be stirred in such a way to take action. As they grew older, the boys would have seen each other less as the demands of their families would have relied on them to contribute their labor. None-the-less, holidays would have afforded the young men to reconnect, sharing a meal of bread with one another as their father's caught up on stories. Jesus' cousin seemed to turn to the wild hippie side, embracing his all-natural diet of honey and roasted locusts while stitching his own clothes from camels' hides. The desert sun tightened John's skin, causing early crow's feet to line his stern eyes. A wild donkey of a man yet one who spoke truthfully of God's convictions during a Greek influenced Roman world. A sort of hell, fire & brimstone type of guy calling out senators & governors on their corrupt standards. Many believed John to be odd, a radical, while some found him intriguing, like a prophet who was anointed by God, baptizing people into repentance. Jesus begins His eulogy by taking up his cousin's mantle. John the Baptist' ministry is interrupted.

Interrupted. The disciples are in a place of pure passion, on an all-time high of experiencing great miracles, of being instruments of hope and healing. They had just returned from mountain top experiences, eager to share with Jesus all the amazing miracles that had happened. They needed to reconnect with their Teacher, their leader whom they admired and lived for. The disciples wanted Jesus to be proud of their accomplishments.

Jesus' world crashes with the crafty murder of his closest cousin, the very man who had baptized him and Jesus esteemed by telling others that no greater person had ever been born before. Jesus' life is interrupted w/ pain & grief as He mourns the loss of his murdered cousin, a man of integrity whose life is snuffed out by corruption & scandal.

John the Baptist's ministry is interrupted, leaving many confused and wondering about God's goodness. Their worlds collide in an astronomical storm of all-time high emotions and low at this very moment, in this one little section of scripture. Hungry. Emotionally spent. Tapped out. Can you imagine it? Can you picture how the disciples were like a demanding toddler that follows their parent around who has the flu and can't wait for a snack? The miserable parent begs for nap time to happen. Just a little rest.

Some of us beg for a break, just a moment of peace, while others of us beg for just one bite, one moment of glory to be a part of something bigger, to do something great. Some of us have a dream, a loved one, a ministry ripped from our very hands that we believed God had promised. What happened? Why now, God? Why? How could You? I'm exhausted and have nothing else to give.

Why are You interrupting me? My Life? Why are you leaving me hungry? Why are you placing people in my life who have it all right now?

Interrupted. We are constantly interrupted by Life and environment. As Americans, we're barraged with 5second cell phone notifications. About 95% of all adult Americans own a cell phone. With that, 26 billion texts are sent each day in the U.S. by 277million people. An electronic device we buy has permission to have exclusive rights to our personal attention at any time during the day, even in the night.

Most texts are read in 5secs. Approximately 781 billion text messages are sent every month, equaling to about 9.3 trillion a year, breaking down to 94 text messages a day, per person. Each person interacts with 33,834 text messages in an entire year. We interrupt our lives using more texts than internet now. (*textrequest.com*)

Interrupted.

Do you feel interrupted by simple, every day text messages? A constant email flow in your Inbox? What about your personal life, do you carry the weight of taxiing decisions to make?

"Is it time to place mom in a nursing home? When is the right time to pull the plug, to let go of all hope? Should I change career paths? What do I do with my time now that I am retired? My college degree feels meaningless, when will that dream job open up for me?

When can I have a full night's rest from this colicky baby? When can I be raised up in ministry? How do I share my faith with my boss?". So many questions. So many interruptions.

Interrupted & Hungry; barely noticed when we skim through this area of scripture. Yet, this place, this positioning of hunger caused from interruptions is about to be satisfied in an impossible way.

INTERRUPTED

During all the spilled stories, what kind of condition are the disciples in during the middle of Mark 6, verse 31? What is Jesus hungry for?

Who can you relate with most; the disciples in a season of rejoicing, Jesus in the mess of grieving good-bye's, or like John the Baptist, everything hoped for is now gone, leaving confusing thoughts?

Like uninvited party-crashers, the disciples interrupt Jesus' need to grieve. Jesus listens for as long as humanly possible and finally raises a hand of enough, interrupting the disciples exciting stories of transformation. Talk about what feels interrupted in your life right now.

What you are hungry for?

Why would God allow these two vastly different worlds of joy & grief to collide at this very moment?

EXPECTATIONS

"Come with me, by yourselves, to a quiet place and get some rest. So they went away by themselves in a boat to a solidary place. But many who saw them leaving recognized them and ran on foot from all the towns and got there ahead of them. When Jesus landed and saw a large crowd, he had compassion on them because they were like sheep without a shepherd. So he began teaching them many things."

Vs 32-34

magine the leaders, Jesus' disciples unwinding after several weeks on the road, not sleeping in their own beds, eating God knows what at each home they stayed in. Worn out from simply giving so much of themselves to hurting and tormented, troubled and hopeless people. Jesus promised words echoing in their minds, "Come away with me, by yourselves to a quiet place, and get some rest." (Mark 6:31). The rocking motion of the waves unwinding the tension in their sore bodies. The shoreline becoming more distant as they set sail allowing their thoughts to slow down. Hearing the lapping waves soothes their tired souls like a child's lullaby. Something about the Captain standing at the helm of their ship gave their weary minds permission to rest. No phones, no emails, no text messages to check. Off in the distance, they awaken from their sleep-like trance. Noise. Like the hum of locusts on a summer evening, fills the air, increasing in decibels to a near deafening roar.

Thousands of eager faces press in for a better look. Their ship of solitude pulls into port, deck hands grab ropes securing their destination like a nail in the coffin. The disciple's faces are filled with disbelief as thousands of anxious faces offer nervous smiles of excitement. All eyes look to the Captain. Crest-fallen & sullen, the disciples can't believe their luck. This...this was supposed to be about THEM! Their time, their moment to belong, a little one-on-one, vay-cay down the drain. A small flicker of hope rose up that Jesus would assert Himself by sticking up for his boys declaring that his disciples needed some R&R, a little down time of rest and relaxation. Eyes filled with hope of different motivations lock on Jesus from every direction.

Tension mounts, leaving little room for a full breath of air. The Captain scans the horizon, his thoughts shrouded behind bushy eyebrows. His mouth opens, moistened by the salty sea air. All grows still as breath is abated, held still by the need to hear his voice. The sun-warmed tanned skin softens as words of gentle rain fill the sky. Their boat nearly capsizes as people climb in for a closer look and better seat. An afternoon sun shower glistens as he speaks, parting the gray sky, giving song to the birds. Truly, a miracle has happened. The Captain of their soul is genuinely glad as his warm eyes greet each person with a smile. The disciples let out a groan. Here we go again. Their retreat just went down the drain.

Ever felt like one of these people in the crowd, full of expectation in seeing someone famous? Snap Chat lit your phone up motivating you to dip from work early, Instagram pics of miracles fill your screen growing hope in your soul that just maybe there was room for another miracle in your life. Scrambling to find parking in an already filled lot, you pull in behind the fish taco hut hoping your car isn't in the tow away zone of the dumpster. Just maybe this Jesus would be interested in healing your gimp leg, your bummed soul. There's a sea of faces running for the dock, the Tweets directed them where to fly to find the landing strip before Jesus' projected arrival. The crowd has expectations. You have expectations.

What about the disciples, can you relate to their well-earned expectation? Did Jesus seriously lead them on, promising a personal retreat of alone time and then, wham, out of nowhere appears all these needy people? Needy, sniveling faces. Just looking for the next hand out. A bunch of parasitic miracle seekers. The disciples are worn out & hungry, no bread stowed on the boat, nothing stuffed in the pockets. Hunger wrecked its havoc leaving behind any pleasantries of hello's washed out to the sea. Irritated by the enormous crowd, the boys were in no mood to play. Not an ounce of interest resides in their weary bodies to rise and begin teaching alongside Jesus. No inkling that just maybe this was their Dream Team moment of healing the sick together. This get away was supposed to be a private event on a private beach, away from everyone. A sort of inclusive Members Only Beach Club just for them. Jesus, all to themselves. They had clear expectations.

Jesus displays an expectation of how he wants to grieve after receiving the painful news of how his radically religious cousin had been decapitated while in prison. Scouring the shoreline, He locates a boat, climbs in with his closest friends and rows out to a remote location, free of distractions, free of interruptions. Jesus expects to grieve privately,

14

away from the public spotlight. Thoughts crowding his mind, Jesus ponders the stories from his disciples in the rocking boat, and his words of instruction to only take a shepherd's staff on their missionary trip. Clear expectations of empty pockets, empty bank accounts, with no bread, traveling in pairs yet definitely with a staff in their hand.

"Take nothing for yourselves for the journey, except a staff..."

Jesus went around teaching from village to village. Calling the Twelve to him, he sent them out 2 by 2 and gave them authority over unclean spirits. These were his instructions: Take nothing for the journey with you except a staff – no bread," no wallet, no money deposited to your bank accounts, you can wear your shoes but no extra clothes. When you're invited into a home, stay there in that one house until you're ready to leave. If any town or neighborhood won't listen to you, shake the dust off your sandals as a testimony against them. They went out and preached that people should turn to God. They dispersed many demons and anointed the sick with oil and healed them, restoring them to their original condition & purpose.

Author's word insertion of expansion

Mark 6:7-12

Personal items for their road trip? Not a chance! Pics of their girlfriend tucked away in a hidden wallet with some extra cash? Nope! Certainly, no bread. Jesus sends His disciples into the nearby towns with no means of support, we might call them old-fashioned missionaries. Only difference is they weren't raising support before going out in the field. No trail mix baggies, no beef jerky strips for the road, no gas station pit stops along the way. Don't take any extra clothes, no extra money. No bread. This doesn't sound like a caring friend, let alone a loving God. Can you imagine telling one of your closest friends to go on a road trip and take no extra anything? No money. No bread. How were they to feed themselves? Of all the things they are directed to take, they're told to take a staff. Doesn't seem to do much good; can't swipe a credit card with a shepherd's staff at a local convenience store. An impractical item to pack for the cool, desert evenings. A staff certainly wasn't going to produce any manna from heaven to fill their bellies. No bread. Sounds like the disciples were sent out with no support except good wishes. They were completely vulnerable.

"Poof, you can heal and preach to all the audience you can muster up, boys. But no bread for the journey. No extra change of clothes. No money to purchase needed items, you're gonna be roughing it, no GlamCam for you!"

These hard-core disciples were sent with the complete belief that hospitality would offer its friendly hand. As they entered each unknown village, looking very much like fish out of water, the duty, or obligation was for the elder or a head of a prominent household to take care of the needs of such a lonely sojourner, offering food, water, shelter and rest.

Why would Jesus do such a thing, to seemingly empower his closest followers to do great miracles yet possess so little to take care of themselves? Arrive in town completely empty handed, looking like a desert-born shepherd looking for a free Happy Meal? Doesn't sound like a loving Teacher but rather a harsh slave-driver demanding impossible living conditions. Unless Jesus foreknew that their interruption would create an expectation of hunger within the communities. Could it be that Jesus saw the greater picture, perceiving nothing within the disciples themselves would have impressed folks to hear their message? Nothing about their sweat-stained desert clothing would have impressed a crowd to gather and witness such miracles. Rather, the miracle was within them, given to them by Jesus by his spoken word.

They would have to rely on the benevolence of the people to take care of their most basic needs with only a staff as proof of their discipleship. A 7ft long stick to protect themselves from stray dogs looking for a leg to chase. A carved pole in their hand to steady their weary pace for when they grew tired on the pot-hole riddled road. Moses had carried a staff. Jacob had carried a staff. Now these men, who were professing to follow the savior of the world, were carrying a staff. Proficient as a weapon in defense against a predator, their staff was a picture of comfort and authority. Easily perceived from a distance, their staff was a symbol of having the right to lead, even if it were a bunch of smelly sheep.

A staff could save any sheep who had wondered away and got caught in the bushes, preventing the shepherd from the injury of piercing thorns. A staff scooped many a stray sheep from lost ledges of cliff diving. Yes, the shepherd's staff is the one thing Jesus tells his disciples to take. A hired shepherd ran the potential of treating his sheep harshly, being mean, driving them hard, perhaps even beating a few when tempers ran hot and patience ran thin. A paid shepherd had no skin in the game except to do the job and not an ounce more.

A paid shepherd would never place their life on the line to snatch sheep from the jaws of a wolf or bear. After all, the shepherd needed to work the next day; no missing fingers please.

An expectation for hot-headed bar-brawling James to become a shepherd. Impulsive Peter to quit running amuck by carrying a shepherd's staff instead of a fishing pole. Friendly, people-pleasin' Philip walks roads full of strangers with a joo-joo stick in his hands. Bribe-ridden Matthew leaves his prospering turn-a blind-eye sort of business to go out with empty pockets. An expectation to receive from the strangers around them, humbling their educated hands.

Expectations. Crest-fallen, disappointed disciples. Jesus, shocked at loss. Thousands of hungry souls. All a little tapped out, all in need of food.

Hunger builds as expectations fall.

EXPECTATIONS

Describe a time you were so empty, so hungry, and felt other people were more important than your own needs?

Talk about why the shepherd's staff may have been symbolic for the disciples.

Describe an expectation that turned into a disappointment. How did this make you feel?

What have been some missed moments of stuffing back a compassionate response to someone else's need while being wrapped up in your own world?

Imagine yourself as one of the people in the crowd, hoping to catch a glimpse of Jesus, yet not quite sure what to expect. Compassionate eyes lock with yours, everything about his face says, "I'm glad you're here!"

What feelings are flooding your soul as you picture yourself being seen by Jesus?

PRACTICUM

"By this time it was late in the day, so his disciples came to him. "This is a remote place, and it's already very late. Send the people away so they can go to the surrounding countryside and villages and buy themselves something to eat. But Jesus answered, 'You give them something to eat.' They said to him, 'That would take 8months wages! Are we to go and spend that much on bread and give it to them?"
Vs 35-37

The typical church service time of 60 minutes shoved right out the door, Jesus spoke for hours, tenderly explaining in detail God's love for them with broad gestured hand movements. The crowd sits, chewing grass blades between their teeth, spellbound and mesmerized by his every word. The disciples settle back in the boat trying to nod off, feigning indifference as their eyes closed. Their nonchalance of tuning out the crowd only seems to drive the volume up louder. Reluctant to admit, their own ears greedily soak up the rain within their own thirsty souls. So much for a private audience.

Compassion motivates Jesus, energizing him as the sun begins to set in the western sky. Long shadows appear as jackets are pulled out, much like a San Francisco evening. The people settle in, comfortably leaning on one another, huddled in for warmth. They were going nowhere.

At the end of their rope, irritated disciples clamor up to Jesus, shoulder checking a few on their quest to rescue their Captain who appeared to forget about his crew. Believing the sun played havoc on his memory, the disciples press their cause to dispense the needy crowd. In their gruffest, no-nonsense tone, they interrupt Jesus, "We're out in the middle of nowhere, it's late, the sun is going down, these people need to leave and go get themselves some grub from the local gas station 'cause there's no fast food in sight. In case you forgot about us when you saw all these people, we have been starving. Pete forgot to pack granola bars for our trip. Breakfast cinnamon rolls was the last thing we ate. Maybe one of the boys grabbed a fish taco, but man, we need to get out of here. Tell these people to go away, find their own food."

James & John cross their arms over barrel chests, they were done entertaining the people and their Captain needed to remember why he pulled into port. Planting their feet wide in bouncer-like fashion, scowls ran across their broad foreheads making a formidable Thor-like stance. These boys meant business.

Jesus peers intently into the fishermen's seasoned eyes noticing the nickname of notoriety as Sons of Thunder written all over their faces. Voice firm yet soft, like one in full control, Jesus commands the staunch men, "You feed them."

Completely caught off guard at the ridiculous request, James & John fall into toddler-like tantrum with arms unlocking into a thrown wide expression of disbelief.

"Are you kidding me? Eight months, Jesus! 8mos of hard, back-breaking work would feed these parasites who came looking for a handout! While you've been ignoring us, I've been counting every one of those 5,000 sniveling faces. Matthew already did the math an hour ago while you just keeping chattering along.

"At $7.25 an hour, and a 10hr day of $72.50 @ 6days a week, equaling 211 workdays, equals a paycheck of $15, 297.50, round that bad boy up to $15, 300. Because we're out in the middle of no-where land, tack on another $5k for front door delivery, that jacks up the total to about $20k." Face mottled in anger, the spray zone widening, James gives full vent, contorting his face in a sarcastic scowl. Glancing over, "Hey Judas, yo' money bags, do we have $20k sitting in our traveler's account? 'Cause last I saw we were in the red, bottom lined at zero dollars 'cause Jesus told us not to raise any money for our save-the-world road tour!" Turning back to Jesus, raising the pitch of a mimicking voice, "Take no bread with you. Remember that, Jesus?" Completing his rage of pent up rejection boiling up from the setting sun, James wheels around, pointing a finger at Jesus in accusation, "In case you forgot, I might be a fisherman but I'm also a businessman. I've ran my company for years before you blew into town. I can do the math. These people aren't worth twenty thousand dollars for a one-night stand of little snack cakes!".

Fuel abated, the other disciples shift nervously from foot to foot. Sure, they all felt the same, but no one was going to lose their top over it. Deeply disappointed. Bone weary with hunger gnawing like a ravaging wolf in their own bellies, the disciples are completely at a loss of Jesus' command to feed five thousand people. They were all in over their heads. James & John's reputation as hotheads reveals itself in true colors like a middle eastern hot-bedded war eruption. Awkward silence fills the air. Lines drawn in the sand. A tense game of chess showdown. James backs Jesus in a corner with a Checkmate.

Personal retreat Interrupted. Expectations of being fed themselves with just their personal friends around a campfire gone. Ladies & gentlemen, grief time has been placed on hold; please come back another time. Empty souls so hungry to hear words of hope. Is this a super-focused work-a-holic Jesus, neglecting his most valuable friendships to people please a crowd to feed his own narcissistic ego? The disciples, waiting for the sermon to wrap up, having hours to count and recount all the bobbing heads in the audience. Light-headed dizziness as sugar levels drop leaving most in near diabetic coma.

As if every emotional deficit were a topping from the local froyo shop wasn't enough, Jesus barely stops the momentum of his teaching to offer an ever-deepening dilemma. It's a practicum moment for the disciples. You figure out a way to feed all these people. An impossible task with so many empty bellies. Jesus looks at the crowd and feels compassion for the beautiful sheep, he wants to be close, spend the rest of his day with them. The disciples look at the crowd and see inconvenience, not an ounce of compassion resides in their souls for the people going out of their way just to catch a glimpse of Jesus. Jesus

Christ, a glamorous super star, just lovely.
Groupies, please go away, the show is over.

Where were the staffs they carried from town
to town? When did the song leave their heart of
praising God for all the miracles? The desire to
heal and set people free washed down the drain,
long forgotten.

Nice try Jesus, this isn't exactly the best time to
teach us an "Aha" moment. Why would you ask
me to empty my already empty bank account to
give a simple meal to others?

The Practicum? It's a perfect basketball lay up
to score some points. "You feed them."

PRACTICUM

Why would Jesus ask his disciples to give of something they didn't have?

Even with a grieving heart, Jesus' response was compassion as he healed the sick and taught the people. The disciples had been given the same authority to heal. Offer some ideas as to why they didn't reach out to the crowd.

Read 2Corinthians 5:18-20. We have all been given the ministry of reconciliation, as an ambassador representing Jesus, sent to restore right relationships back to their original design and purpose. We have been given the same ability. What holds you back in speaking words that can heal?

Imagine yourself being sent out to live in your world with a shepherd's staff. What will the people who know you best say about you?

Jesus doesn't enter the argument with his disciples, setting clear boundaries by remaining focused on what mattered most, enjoying being with the people. Discuss ways you can navigate challenging people or relationships by remaining present instead of withdrawing.

INVENTORY

"Jesus asked, 'How many loaves of bread do you have? Go, and see.' When they found out, they said, 'Five loaves and two fish.'"

Vs. 38

I n the same, steady rhythm of a softly lapping wave, Jesus asks his outraged and offended friend one question: How much bread do you have? Go, find out. Jesus looks away, continuing his teaching. He knows his young myth-like Thor will rise to the challenge to prove him wrong. Unspoken words filter through James' heart,

"Check. We're not in a check mate. This is a "check" moment, a chance to find another way. Back me in the corner with a check mate and you'll see the impossible made possible. I Am Captain. I know where the sun sets. Time ticks forth from My Hand. I know how many hairs are on all five thousand of these precious people. My Breath is in their lungs. This moment, this moment now is for my Bread that will fill their bellies. I Am the Bread of Life. You who are hungry and have no

28

money in your pockets, come to Me. Take and eat all the bread you want, even though you can afford it and can't barter for it. Eat from My Hand and you will never be hungry again. I fully satisfy and leave no one in want. Open wide your mouth and eat greedily until you cannot move from the table. I AM Bread. Take an inventory of your own capacity. When you find yourself empty handed, come back to Me with the little bit you scrounged up and place it in My Hand. It's not about you, my fired-up friend. I Am generous. I will fill all the bellies here because I care about their souls. I feel their hunger in the pangs of my own belly. I know you are hungry. I feel your hunger as my own. You will survive this moment even while feeling empty. I AM will never leave you out in the middle of nowhere. I Am able. Go, take a closer look, go mingle with the people, brush up against them smelling their body as your own. Go, ask questions, look our people in their eyes, hear their voices, notice the 5o'clock shadow on the men's faces. They are tired just like you, working long and hard all day long. They came out here to see Me, to hear Me, to just get a little something to feed their soul so they can continue this journey here on earth. Go and find some bread, you're not as empty as you believe. The little bit you discover, come place it in My Hands. Seeing this as a chess game? Then, Check.

At least 5thousand and 13 identified people in the crowd. Exactly how long did it take for the 12 men to search through 5,ooo people before coming back with an answer? Imagine the ruckus, the "excuse me's", "pardon me, I didn't mean to step on your toe", sorry I yelled in your ear, wait, what was that you said, can you come a little closer?" Walking in and out of the crowd, the disciples were bound to start smelling like the people. They would have noticed the bags under the eyes, dark circles of restless nights, hollowed-out cheeks from meager households. No hair, lots of hair, no teeth, lots of pearly whites, tall, short, round, brown, light brown, white, dark, super hairy arms, perhaps missing fingers from work related injuries. Brown eyes, hazel, anxious eyes, indifferent looks. Five thousand people later, they were well familiar with the crowd. Kind hands began reaching out to lay a soft touch on shoulders. Lack of eye contact shifts to longer moments of being seen. Good jokes are cracked, and begrudging smiles begin to break the stone-faced, stressed out disciples. These people aren't so bad after all.

Two small fish, ever a reminder for the disciples of Jesus' promise to make them fishers of mankind. All four Gospels later written would record Jesus' intent for ministry; "Come, Follow Me and I will make you fishers of men."

"I will equip you, Luke! As a physician you will heal people's souls like never before!"

Matthew, known for ripping off people and taking bribes, "oh Matthew, you will want to give to make people whole. An entire generation who's uncomfortable going to church will come to your home to hang out and hear about Me, the Bread of Life!"

"I will teach you and show you by example how to interact with the world around you. There will be no effort to convince someone to follow Me. As you follow Me, you will look like Me, smell like Me, speak like Me, heal like Me, restore relationships like Me, offer hope like Me."

"Then Jesus said to Philip, "Where should we buy bread for these people to eat?" He asked this only to test him, for he already had in mind what he was going to do. Philip answered, "8months wages would not be enough bread for each one to have a bite!" Another of his disciples, Andrew, Peter's brother, spoke up, "Here is a boy with 5small barley loaves and 2small fish, but how far will they go with so many?"

John 6:5-9

John shares a different perspective and offers the scoop to privy conversations. Maybe not wanting to account his wrathful reputation as being the brother of hot-headed James, the 2men were very much 2peas in one pod. John rather, shines the light on Jesus intentionally testing Philip to locate bread. Jesus already has a plan of action played out yet prods Philip to dig a little deeper. Philip is kind of like this good guy from the same town as Peter & Andrew and has a seemingly strong concern for his friend Nathanael who's a clean-cut sort of man who never went to jail. Birds of a feather, flock together; this is a mild-mannered Philip with intellect that's trying to wrap his mind around Jesus' outlandish request. Rather than raising a brawl, he enters in a type of gentle ping pong negotiator type of chat with Jesus, trying to reason with him.

In the original written language of this account by sons of Thunder John, a word "pi-rad-zo" delves us to see the motive behind Jesus' bread question. 'Piradzo' literally means to test objectively as an endeavor, to examine. Jesus is asking Philip to test him in a way as to bring out the best in Philip, not to harm him. Another words, it wasn't a personal attack on Philip to find the answer, not a trick to embarrass him but to engage him in such a way as to go and seek the answer. Philip has this gentle, yet incredulous reasoning with Jesus that even if enough money was scraped together, there still wasn't enough for more than a mouthful. Philip is using his reasoning and intellect to figure out a solution.

Up walks eager Andrew, proud of his prized find of a small child with 5 barley rounds of bread and 2 small salty fish. "Drop the microphone, above and beyond, boom baby, I found some fish!" Even with his proud prize, even Andrew is inclined to use his reasoning to figure out a way to make the food happen. Super spiritual Andrew, ready to exercise a little more faith than the others, believing there had to be bread somewhere. Andrew had way more experience tucked up under his belt in first being a disciple of John the Baptist before leaving the team for the new spiritual advisor in town. Andrew is willing to take a closer look while carrying the death of his favorite coach in his heart. Andrew is a man also grieving, baffled by the unanswered expectations of God's kingdom to restore all social justice wiped away by a seductive dance. Andrew stifles his need to grieve and has a willingness to move forward, scanning the crowd for much needed bread.

Andrew, previous follower of Wild Camel Man, brother to impulsive, risk-taker Peter, locates a small child with an inventory of 5 rounds of 8inch circular barley bread in the crowded area. Barley bread from the poor, a millet based dense circle of nutrition baked with one person in mind and maybe a friend if you felt like sharing. Mingling with the poor, no high money roller's here. Two small fish, a typical Palestinian meal for everyday people along with some chunks of bread from a child.

Andrew discovers he has a backbone, a voice that won't be drowned out by his outgoing brother. Andrew has hope that 5loaves will feed a few; then what?

A child with 5loaves of bread, perhaps for his family, most like peddling sales at a young age. No bribery if offered, no lollipop exchange. The child willingly gives his 5 rounds of poor man's bread, and with wide-eyed wonder, is escorted to front row tickets with Jesus. The next generation is watching the Teacher intently, taking inventory of the vast crowd around him with child-like innocence that the impossible was about to happen.

Jesus interrupts the child's meal with an expectation that his disciples will allow the practicum to touch their hearts, opening their minds to inventory what was most important. The Bread.

INVENTORY

There are 492 references to bread in the bible. Talk about the importance of bread.

Poor man's food. Doesn't sound like a lot of potential. Why is this bread about to become so valuable?

Read John 6:35. Jesus describes himself as being the Bread of Life. Why would Jesus call himself as poor man's food?

Putting yourself in this story, who can you most associate with? James & John, the sons of Thunder, Philip, Andrew, or the young child?

Why the mention of 2 small fish? John 1:40, Matthew 4:19, Luke 5:2 and Mark 1:16-20

Could the fish have been a visual reminder for the disciples to always see the potential in people as hungry and in need of something to satisfy them?

Read Luke 5:1-10. Talk about what you discover.

BREAD

"Then Jesus directed them to have all the people sit down in groups on the green grass. So they sat down in groups of hundreds and fifties. Taking the 5 loaves and 2fish and looking up to heaven, he gave thanks and broke the bread. Then He gave them to his disciples to set before the people. He also divided the 2fish among them all."

Five thousand people directed by 12 ordinary men that were just placed in charge of 416 people, give or take a few. Snap, a commander of 416 precious lives! Dividing that number into a few groups of 50 and another of 100; at least 6pods of swarming, hungry people near sunset per disciple.

"Dude, I had no idea Jesus would have me leading over 400 people! I was good with my dad and my airboat skimming the surface of the sea dragging our nets for fish. Wish my dad could see me now!", lets out a walloping John.

"Yep, looks a lot like the people who lined up to pay their taxes, that line is gonna go right on out the door." declares a Matthew.

"400 people, Jesus? You want me to lead 400 people to areas of grass that are super comfy? Aye, Aye, Captain, I'm on it!"

"How on earth we gonna make 417 pieces of bread happen? Maybe if you made some bread puddin' or somethin', maybe it would stretch." questions a cautious leader, scratching his head in puzzlement.

"Heck ya'!" declares high risk taker Peter, rolling up his sleeves laying out a plan in his determined stride. "Give me 400 more!".

"Hey, it's fiesta time, let the party begin, take a party hat please!", as the optimistic disciple dances around his group passing out piñatas.

5000 people on a remote mountainside next to the sun setting sea. 12disicples with no former experience suddenly in charge of over 400 people looking for green grass. 1 Jesus, 5loaves of bread, & 2 anchovy sized fish. One loaf of bread per one thousand people; outlandish and impossible. The disciples are now ready to get their hands dirty, ready to lead and care for their people even though their hands are empty.

One hundred percent reliance on their Teacher to lead them in a place to sit in a restful position. Relaxed, ready to receive.

Read Psalm 23

Written 1000years earlier, Psalm 23 describes a relationship between 2 people; one as the beneficiary and the other as the Giver, a shepherd and sheep. Sheep tended to stick around in one area, mowing the grass nibs down perfectly unless a shepherd took the lead to find good places to graze. The shepherd is a constant green beret vigilante, on the constant look out for the best interest of his sheep. A shepherd never pushed his sheep hard knowing the stress it would cause on the mothers. Easily agitated and easy pickin' with no incisors to defend themselves, a shepherd was constantly attentive to the needs of his sheep. The rod and staff offered direction to the shepherd's movement, securing the sheep's best interest both in rest and food. Fear simply did not exist with the sheep when their shepherd led them. It's a picture of a loving protector building a table for his sheep, with the table being a barrier between the sheep and an enemy that would try to attack. Nothing could harm the sheep while residing at the table that was supplied with as much food as the sheep wanted to eat. What did the sheep offer in return? Not much, they were completely dependent on the abundance of generosity or lack thereof, from their shepherd, their leader. It's a picture of a loving, enjoyable relationship with one another with nothing in the sheep's ability to gain the affection of the shepherd. Sheep simply couldn't impress a shepherd.

Jesus picks up the 5 loaves of poor man's bread, unashamed of its modesty along with the 2 small fish and looks to heaven with words of, "our Father, who is in heaven, holy & sacred is your name, we beckon Your Presence here, it is Your desire to be here in relationship with your people here on this earth just like it will be completed in heaven. Today, we need You as our daily bread….".

Compassion floods the Shepherd to make certain his people don't pass out on their way home.

Bread to complete their journey, silencing the emptiness they felt in their soul. The ultimate need was bread of God's Presence for their souls. Throughout the old testament, bread represented God's Presence, a fresh loaf baked daily and set in the most holy place. Bread as a memorial to remember God's provision of manna in the desert, melting in their mouths while tasting like sweet honey. The disciples were so focused on the here and now, they couldn't see the needs of the souls around them. An eternal soul that would shed its skin to exist in completion of perfect relationship with their heavenly father. An internal consumption of bread leaving its mark of eternal perspective.

Jesus offers a Eulogy, invoking a benediction while holding the bread and fish. Jesus is talking good about God, *to God*, that God would act in being good to his people because he sees their greatest need.

"Euloge": well-spoken of & acted upon in the original Greek language. When the subject is God, His speaking *is* His action; another way to see it is, *God's speaking & acting are one and the same!* When God is said to bless us, eulogize us, speak well of us, He acts for our good and sees what we need most and not what we desire. The "eulogia" of God is God's action or interference in a person's

life, to bring them to the desired relationship with Himself.

Bread. Given to connect hungry people with a loving and compassionate God.

Do you need to hear this spoken over you? God is already speaking good on your behalf, that you will be in a right relationship with Him. God is looking right at you, right amid this crowd saying, "I see you. I see your hunger. I see what gnaws at your soul. I Am Bread. Come, take all you want. Keep eating until your belly is full. Your pockets are empty, mine are deep. Your spiritual bank account is bankrupt. I see it, *I see you*! Come, take from Me, you who have no money and fill up on a relationship that will sustain your soul."

Plain, ordinary bread. Overlooked and unimpressive barley bread for the average Joe, the everyday Jane. Bread we have no ability to buy.

Our greatest need is eternal Bread we have no practicum to buy, while interrupted by inventoried expectations of cheaply made bread.

BREAD

What proof do we have that God is a compassionate God? (vs. 34)

In verse 34, the people were SEEN. Jesus' response is feeling compassion for them for they had lived their own way and had no one to lead them back to the Great Shepherd.

Describe what goes through your mind that you're "seen".

When was the last time you talked good about God?

Often, we save our eulogies for the dead, spoken during funerals, or at a wedding vow exchange.

Write a eulogy, bragging about God seeing the needs of people and is already in the movement of meeting that need.

You're not just a number lost in a huge crowd. Write another eulogy, bragging about God seeing your deepest need for connection with Him.

SATISFIED

"Jesus broke the bread and kept giving it to his disciples to set before the people. They all ate and were satisfied."

Buffet lines? Not a chance! Reclining, leaning back against one another in relaxed fashion on the soft green grass, the people chatted freely. No effort was needed to get up and walk to a healthy dose of self-serve. Sitting in a position to receive, a little lower than the disciples who walked around them, everything symbolic of their relationship with their heavenly father. They had no extra cash for their spur of the moment countryside outdoor concert. No food in their pockets to share with one another. Nothing, zilch, nada; helpless to bake any fresh bread. Thousands of human bodies strewn across the mountain in lounging form, watching the sunset of brilliant colors dance across the Galilean Sea. Stomachs growled in expectation; they were so hungry! As was the custom of their land, they watch Jesus, curious about the bread in His hand. As a father in a household taking his position at the table, Jesus' lips move in a barely audibly prayer as eyes look up for some unseen connection. The carpenter's rough hands grasp the bread and tear the density, separating in two pieces. Fascinating, just like Home. He offers torn pieces of bread, perfectly in stride with their culture, to the expectant disciples' hands. They, in turn, pile up as much as they can in their arms, returning to their groups of fifty. Back and forth they continue, and Jesus' Hands never seem to tire of tearing the bread. Just like at home when papa would call everyone in the family back together for the evening meal. The barley loafs a main staple of their meal, made their home smell so good. Freshly baked and warmed by the oven, mouths watered in expectation of the soft, sustaining pleasure of being fed. Every …. single…. day. Glorious freshly baked bread filled their bellies day in and day out. Laughter spilled around the table as the family shared their day's events. The town drama, local news of get away sheep running loose causing havoc, the Roman soldiers no nonsense way of marching through their streets making dogs run in fear of their sandaled kicks. Connecting, sharing, listening, being heard and being seen by one another. This indeed was what family felt like. The fresh salty air and beautiful sunset view offers the people to let their minds relax as their bellies are filled with bread, eating as much as they wanted. Like a child in pure innocence eating to their heart's content, no shame in being self-conscience from the scale's weight allowance. Counting carbs not an option, everyone has plenty to eat. As the disciples walk back and forth, the faces become more familiar, names are remembered, as faces smile. Cheeks stuffed themselves, the disciples are amazed the bread never runs out. No worries of someone being left out or going home hungry. The noise begins to rise as hearts are full and bellies are fed. This is what they were made for. Connecting with one another with reliance on their father to provide for them.

"Jesus, full of the holy spirit, returned from the Jordan and was led by the Spirit in the desert, where for forty days he was tempted by the devil. He ate nothing during those days and at the end of them, he was hungry."

Luke 4:1-2

Forty days of no bread before Jesus' ministry even begins.

First Temptation: *"IF* you **ARE** the Son of God, tell this stone to become bread."

IF. At a time of incredible depletion & vulnerability, the enemy boldly questions Jesus' Deity. IF. Sprinkle a little doubt on a hazy day and windshield wipers will do little to clear the vision of path. As if adding insult to injury, the enemy deepens the dagger's plunging words, *"if you ARE…"*

Imagine childhood playground days, the taunting of 'Nany, Nany, boo, boo my mama said to pick the very best one and you are not it!' Remember that childhood taunt? "Who do you say you are? You state your name is Jesus, but who are YOU really? If you are who you say you are, then prove yourself!" Ever felt that way in your workplace, at your school, maybe even in your friendships? The need for approval. Am I likable just the way I am, or do I need to change? Is my fundamental wiring crossed up and I need to change the very nature of who I am just to fit in? This is a socially dynamic and personal attack of judgement against Jesus.

"Who's are you? Where do you come from? Prove you're as good as you say you are! Prove it by picking up a piece of earth, a piece of nothingness and magically turn it into a lucky charmed morsel of bread."

A deeper challenge still, is the implication in the Tempter's question; do things on your own Jesus! "You tell this stone to become bread. You got the raw end of the deal, born into poverty with a bunch of half-brother's and sister's, the whole town whispers about your mother's infidelity. You came from nothing, you are nothing. You wanna believe you're something special, prove yourself! Prove you're more than nothing from a smelly no-good little town out in the middle of nowhere. You're nothing but trailer trash Jesus, but go ahead, prove yourself! Do what you want to do, be the boss of your dreams, call the shots Jesus and make it happen. Turn these rocks into bread so you can feed your pathetic, desert-starved face!" the snarl dripping in derision as the enemy spits one last venomous punch to Jesus.

Quietly, in full confidence and unraised voice, Jesus answers out of his hunger while standing on the completeness of God's Word. No arguing. No need to prove anything. No self-help get better quick solutions. Simply the sound authority and finality of His Father's Words. "There is no "if" because I Am fully man, fully human and God says living on bread alone will never fully satisfy me. I and the Father are one. Apart from Him, I can do nothing. It is my Father's good pleasure to pour out my life for the ransom of many. I will stand on my heavenly Father's word and do nothing from selfish motives. I and the Father are One, therefore I am perfectly secure in who I am, where I came from and Whom I'm connected to. Our relationship is perfect."

Jesus, fully human and incredibly hungry answers the self-doubt with scriptures, "It is written, man does not live on bread alone." (vs 3-4)

"Gather up the fragments that nothing may be lost. The disciples gather 12 basketfuls of bread and fish."

A fragment of bread, anything larger than the size of an Israeli grown olive, collected, picked up and stored for later, just like what they did back home. Breadcrumbs. Never discarded, never wasted nor thrown out. Gathered up and saved for an evening snack or afternoon munchie. Relationship with the Father collected and stored moments of reflecting on Jesus' words. When self-doubt or derision lifted its ugly head later, breadcrumbs were sure to chase them away. Promises and provisional reminders that God loved them and when they felt hunger rise, to remember how good the bread tasted. 12 baskets filled to the brim, a basket for each disciple to carry. They had poured out so much, had served others to the point of exhaustion, had their personal retreat washed down the drain but something happened in the course of the day. What they thought they had wanted most was satisfied by connecting people with one another and with their heavenly Father.

Energized by the bread, they stare in wonder at the abundance. 5 loaves of bread per 5 thousand people; Impossible! Yet, here they were carrying 12 baskets full of breadcrumbs. They had given so little and yet their hands were full. Their bellies were full. Everyone was content, even a little sleepy.

"Man, I'm such an idiot, why didn't I believe?" says a contemplative Peter. Even money bags Judas is left wondering how so much was given on so little a budget.

"Piñatas full of bread for everyone, did you see what Jesus did? That was dope!" grabbing their baskets, busy gathering leftovers for the journey still ahead, reflective disciples are quieted like a child with a full belly.

God, a Generous Giver. Jesus connecting people Home. Bread given to satisfy souls.

Bread symbolizing the Presence of God in relationship with us. Much like a child, we have no money to purchase any food. We're invited to sit at our Father's table, where He takes the bread, speaking good about our relationship with him as he tears the bread into chunks. His Hand brushes against ours in tenderness as warm bread is pressed into our open, receiving hand. We can eat as much as we want, and like an unabashed child, we consume the soft bread, relishing its taste. We hear our Father's voice encouraging us to eat more. Our bellies are so full, we're about to burst. Heavy with bread and feeling sleepy, the stories of shared moments flow around the table about our day, connecting our hearts. Our Father listens and we notice He is delighted, absolutely thrilled, we're sharing a meal together.

BREAD torn and given to you, to me. An offering of peace & friendship at the expense of Jesus.

Won't you come and stay awhile?

Satisfied by Bread from the Shepherd's Inventory of heavenly abundance, with a Practicum Expectation to Interrupt God with your hunger.

SATISFIED

The people had "as much bread as they wanted" and also, "when they had enough to eat…"

What does this seem to imply about God?

After reading this, describe what bread (communion) means to you now.

How did Jesus combat self-doubt and the temptation to do things his own way?

What kind of breadcrumbs are stuffed in your pockets right now?

How do you feel about interrupting God with your hunger for Bread?

References

Jesus feeds the 5000

Mark 6:30-44   John 6:1-13   Matthew 13:13-21

Setting for this miracle, The Sea of Galilee   Matthew 4:12-13

Calling of the disciples   Matthew 4:18-22

Instructions being sent out   Matthew 10:1-14   Mark 6:7-13

John the Baptist description   Matthew 3:1-16

textrequest.com   Stats of text message usage

Traditional shepherd's staff was 6 – 9 feet long.

Fishers of men   Matthew 4:19, Mark 1:16-20, Luke 5:2, John 1:40

John the Baptist's disciple was Andrew, the brother of Peter John 1:35-40

Andrew brought Peter, his brother, to Jesus. John 1:41-42

Philip is from the same town as Simon Peter & Andrew   John 1:44

Philip recruits Nathanael who was hanging out under a fig tree and Jesus describes as having no deceit, no guile. John 1:45-48

Pi-rad-zo; to test objectively as in an endeavor, to entice, examine.   Spiros Zodhiates Hebrew-Greek Key Study Bible, NASB June 1990

Eulogemenos/Euloge: well-spoken of, acted upon; when the subject is God, then God's speaking & acting are the same. Spiros Zodhiates Hebrew-Greek Key Study Bible, NASB June 1990

200 denari = $36

Traditionally, 3loaves of bread fed a man, his family and 1guest.

1loaf of bread was given to prisoners as their daily food Jeremiah 37:21

492 passages regarding BREAD in the bible.   Medium.com

Psalm 23 written approx. 1040-970 BC or 1000yrs earlier before Christ   quora.com

"Thor" from a Norse legend myth.

"GlamCam" = glamping. Luxurious camping.

Isaiah 55:1-2 "Ho! Everyone who thirsts, come to the waters; And you who have no money come, buy and eat. Come buy wine and milk without money and without cost. Why do you spend money on what is not bread, and your wages for what does not satisfy? Listen carefully to me, eat what is good, and delight yourself in abundance." Spiros Zodhiates Hebrew-Greek Key Study Bible, NASB June 1990

Bread was the essential, basic food. So basic was it that in Hebrew "to eat bread" and "to have a meal" in the same thing. Bread was treated with great respect and many rules existed to preserve that reverence. Any crumbs of over the size of an olive were expected to be gathered, and never simply discarded. Bread was never to be cut, but always broken. The poor ate barley bread, the rich the bread of wheat.

To make the heavy barley bread rise, women use very strong millets, and barley yeast. The loaves were usually made round, such that one spoke of "a round of bread," or simply "a round." Because bread would become moldy very soon, one would only bake enough for a day or two. Bread and fish were a common meal. This is illustrated by the miracle of the loaves and the fishes, as well as the meal at the lakeside in Galilee where Christ prepared fish for them over a charcoal fire. The Sea of Galilee had great quantities of fish; and fish were also gotten from the Mediterranean Sea. Since fish soon turned bad, it was often salted.

https://hcscchurch.org

It was customary in the ancient home for the father of the household to open a meal by taking a loaf of bread, giving thanks, breaking it, and distributing it to the members present (cf. Billerbeck IV, 620ff.). Evidences of this can be seen in the service of the Lord's Supper when "Jesus took bread, and blessed, and broke it, and gave it to the disciples" (Matt 26:26), which procedure was taught by Paul in his statements about the communion service (1 Cor 11:23, 24). This pattern was followed when Jesus fed the 5,000 (John 6:11). *Biblegateway.com*/resources Bibliography R. A. Macalister, *The Excavation of Gezer II* (1912), 42, 43; J. B. Pritchard, *Ancient Near Eastern Texts* (1955); J. P. Free, *Archaeology and Bible History*, 5th ed., rev. (1956), 76; W. Foerster," TDNT, II, 590-599; H. L. Strack and P. Billerbeck, *Kommentar zum Neuen Testament*, IV (1965), 620-622.

There are at least seven words referencing bread in the Hebrew language version of the Old Testament and three Greek words referring to it in the New Testament.
Mentioned at least 492 times in the original languages of the Bible.
The children of Israel were miraculously feed with "bread from heaven" or Manna as the wandered for forty years before entering the Promised Land (Exodus 16). This food initially symbolized God's love and care for his people, in spite of their sins, and an omer of it was placed inside the Ark of the Covenant (Exodus 16:32 - 34). Jesus revealed the full meaning of Manna when he stated it was a reference to him.
Additionally, in the Bible, bread symbolized Jesus the Messiah and the eternal life he offers to those willing to follow him with their whole heart (John 6:32 - 35, 41, 50 - 51). The unleavened version of this staple was used during Christ's last Passover represented his willingness to offer his own body as a sacrifice for our sins and to make our healing possible (Matthew 26:26, 1Corinthians 11:23 - 30).
https://www.biblestudy.org/bible-study-by-topic/bread-in-the-bible.html

Exodus 40:23 "the bread of his Presence (lit. of His Face in Hebrew)

Bread, the staff of life, was used in the worship of God, primarily through tabernacle (then later temple) services to symbolize the Eternal's presence (Exodus 25:30, Leviticus 24:5 - 9).

Special Thanks to my brave chariot ridin' inner circle of friends who remind me of God's promises and comfort. Their brave steps compel me to forge a few of my own!

My greatest encourager and knight in shining armor husband, who kept walking by asking to read this study. You always believe in me.

For Amber & Diane who nodded their heads in agreement that I could write this study for our women at Journey Fellowship; thank you for wings to fly.

Obviously to Microsoft, Amazon & Canva offering technique palettes that give Indie writers a chance to be seen.

My friends enthusiastically posting FB pics of bread & text msgs of, "I can't wait for your new book!"

My Jesus, who is my Bread, my Life, my absolute saving grace. Never taking Your Eyes off me, You have saved me countless times.

About the Author

Steeped in ministry nearly 30yrs, Christina Gallegos still scratches her head in wonder of how that can be when she claims to be the golden age of 29yrs.

Born & raised in sunny south Florida with ever deepening Texan roots, Christina received recognition for writing during her middle school years. Marked by family difficulty, she was accommodated through the state foster & legal system. Overcoming a propensity for social failure, Christina offers words of encouragement for beaten down souls.

Married to her teenage crush Mario, together they have raised 4 incredible sons and spoil their young grandson along with chasing their newly adopted rescue dog, Archie.

A pastor's wife whose childhood wish was to become the first nun cardiologist, Christina lives in Texas making fresh salsa while cruising the beach in her jeep for the best fishing spot.

Made in the USA
Middletown, DE
07 February 2022

60706326R00045